Singing in the
LIFE BOATS

SOME POEMS, RAMBLES, AND RANTS...AND A FEW LYRICS

Jerry Lagadec

"Life is a shipwreck, but we must not forget to sing in the lifeboats."

Voltaire

SINGING IN THE LIFE BOATS
SOME POEMS, RAMBLES, AND RANTS...AND A FEW LYRICS

iUniverse books may be ordered through booksellers or by contacting:

iUniverse
1663 Liberty Drive
Bloomington, IN 47403
www.iuniverse.com
1-800-Authors (1-800-288-4677)

ISBN: 978-1-4917-9637-5 (sc)
ISBN: 978-1-4917-9636-8 (e)

Library of Congress Control Number: 2016907099

Print information available on the last page.

iUniverse rev. date: 04/30/2016

A FEW WORDS FROM READERS OF "WALKING WITH BASHO"

"Jerry's words invite perspective without pretense; he's always impactful but never preachy. It's relatable philosophy for everyone, from scholar to blue collar."

Katie Trezise [Business Administrator]

"Jerry's poems are not nineteenth century fluff. These are gritty, humorous and honest 'rants' about subjects we all have encountered in real life now. Here is a writer so comfortable with who he is and where he's at that he delivers his poetry with tender humor and pungent sarcasm. The words surprise and delight the reader with "Oh" and "Ah" so we think and feel with an 'ouch' and a chuckle."

Sue Maxwell [Psychotherapist.]

"With '*Walking with Basho*', Jerry Lagadec lets us read between the lines of life. His writing makes us think about the silences between the notes, and the spaces between the words. He has found a way to make us realize a lot of meanings are right in front of us, if we could just learn to be still."

Kris Somers [Musician/Stylist]

"Heartfelt observations regarding life, nature, art, death, and love by a soul who has lived through many experiences. Sometimes rants, sometimes haikus, but always thought provoking and passionate."

Frederick Rose [musician/composer]

"'*Walking with Basho*' is an inspiring and thought provoking book where everyday happenings can seem miraculous."

Marie Plouffe [Librarian-ret.]

"There are riches in the poems, rambles, and rants of this writer's book as it bodies forth the here and now of his experience. You will also find humility in bridging the inevitable gap between the moment and its representation in language as well as a balance between the thing-itself and the emotion behind or inside its perception. He knows and expresses "the sorrow in un-named things that often leaves them un-regarded" and labors to film in words forsythia gone crazy, the last leaf of autumn falling, his wife's frugal gathering of morning glory seeds. Not a still life or a photograph but life in motion. Ideas and feelings do not stand still but pour forth alternative representations in Whitmanesque catalogues, through which "the ordinary is transformed into the intensity of private meaning." Less private than he thinks, perhaps, since his discoveries awaken our own imaginations so that we accept his claim that "you have to try real hard not to become a poet."

Michael Boyd [Professor]

"I would encourage anyone who enjoys poetry to take a look at '*Walking with Basho*'. Many of Jerry's thoughts are profound but in a simplistic way which will resonate with the average reader. My favorite poem 'Waves', jerry states that we should try to 'free ourselves from the learned habit of separating what moments deserve our full attention from those that don't'. It is a poignant yet easy read that will hit home with everyone."

Mike Lucey [UPS driver.]

"I found *Walking with Basho* to be a delightful blend of thought provoking spiritual themes, mixed with two parts sarcastic humor to one part heartfelt sentiment. A great reference if you need a little pep talk...or if you need a quick reality check."

Molly Rovenko Peters [School teacher]

"You don't have to be a poet to enjoy Jerry's carefully crafted collection of poems, rambles, and rants. His candid, often humorous language has sought me to cultivate a more open heart and mind to the simplicities and endless unknowns in my life."

Carol jean L. Lucey [Bookkeeper/Accountant]

"I was not the kind of person that would pick-up a poetry book but once I got to know Jerry I decided to buy his book and give it a try. Now I get it and enjoy it. Jerry's book – "*Walking with Basho*"- is easy to read and I was able to visualize what he was writing about. His poems, rambles, and rants make you laugh, think a bit, and make you say hmmm…what? I look forward to reading his new book."

Lisa Skinner [Tax Custodian]

Contents

Something Before

I like reading wine reviews where you can read the subtleties of various vintages described with such phrases as *"energetic yet graceful," "bold but not boastful"* and my favorite: *"structured yet elegant."* Often the listing of their gustatory overtones include descriptions like *"flamboyant", "oaked", "toasty", "chewy tannins"* and one of my favorites: *"Barnyard,"* indicating that it *"smells like poo".* I read this in a wine article on *Google.* I wanted to immediately go find an example; this may be an indication of what's in store for you in *"Singing in the Lifeboats".*

Now I've never been able to afford the prices of the wines [$55 to $135] in this review. I'm a $12-$15 guy. I know that there are some extremely evolved palates out there who can appreciate the meaning of *"structured yet elegant"* and *"flamboyant" and "toasty".* As for me, I haven't a clue.

This relates to my writing. I know that there are those who possess far more refined, literary "palates" than my own. If I come off as a $12 "bottle" to them, so be it; I really didn't write any of this with the express goal of winning their praise.

I wrote this book with the hope that I would be understood- as much as possible- by "regular" people. I hope this doesn't sound too condescending, but let's face it: say *"poetry"* and many people have unpleasant memories about when they were forced to read it in high school. All that many remember is that they were confused and bored. I guess that by attempting to be more "user friendly", I'm hoping to undo this early negative reaction. If *"Singing in the Lifeboats"* leads to a reconsideration of that early, negative judgment, I'm content.

But don't for a minute assume that I am on some kind of "mission"; I'm not. A traditional greeting in yoga is "Namaste": the "light" in me honors the "light" in you. I believe it's time for us to realize that we are still trapped in that dark dream of fear and anger that has haunted us for millennia. It's time for us to wake up. My simple hope is that by being as honest as possible, I am able to communicate the belief that if we are to move forward toward that "light", we must face those fears and anger and be willing to struggle, to do the work we need to do in order to free ourselves; we must stop depending on outside, organized "structures" that inevitably lead us to view this life through their "filters, no matter how comforting they may be. I do not feel "the answer" resides in some sacred box guarded by the "holy chains" of some religion or philosophy. The "spiritual warrior" does battle with his or her own doubt, with the shadow of death, with weaknesses, with ridicule and threats. All can be embraced and transformed into light.

When I sat down to begin this project, I decided on a few basic guidelines: I wasn't interested in demanding that you solve word and reference puzzles. I wasn't interested in confusing you with complex sentence structures and phrases. Often times those are mental gymnastics. But I don't believe "simple" automatically means "superficial" anymore than "complex" means "profound". The rambles and rants are self explanatory. As humans, we are compelled to share our stories. We unfortunately don't do that much today, we're so busy crunching our necks to view our little screens.

When I was 15, I was infatuated with the blonde in the fourth seat of the second row in Mrs. Higgins English class. As of this writing, I am 73. Out of necessity, my interests have changed as I approach the end of my "lease".

"Singing in the Lifeboats" is my "take" on an alternative to frantic bailing and fearful glances at the threatening "waves."

Peace...and Namaste!

Still Scribbling
[A ramble on resistance]

The latest data is in: there are billions of possible planets out there…many capable of supporting life.

Perhaps some life is crawling out of the ooze on its newly evolved appendages. Perhaps some- from the Spiral Nebulae- is boarding Time Crafts to see if those strange bipeds managed to evolve beyond their hunger and talents for destruction. They did exhibit signs of nascent intelligence- but couldn't seem to control their fondness for slaughtering each other…often… and with great gusto and imagination.

Such has been our history.

I believe that most of the "glues" that have held us together have become increasingly unstable.

That *"Big Daddy in the Sky"* and the *"Old Red Devil down below"* once gave us a sense of …well… importance.

We were watched, judged, and either condemned…or rewarded.

This made sense… and making "sense" out of this existence has always required a certain amount of self hypnosis and the ability to torture the shit out of reason and language… until they give in.

In spite of the endless attempts to explain it to ourselves, the slaughter continues, some intentionally, some just the random butchery of luck and chance.

Any casual perusal of the daily lottery that carries away the innocent and the guilty, the brilliant and the dim, the worst and the best does not speak well for the criteria upon which we can predicate any form of intelligent authority running the clown "show" down below.

It's obvious that our human values: *love, justice, mercy, beauty, kindness, honesty* or any of the other abstractions we have invented to create a more livable world mean nothing in a universe that doesn't give two cosmic turds about whether we survive or not, based on the latest planet data. We need our abstract inventions and we must accept the responsibility of creating them in whatever way we can. No deity is going to do it for us.

We do know one rare absolute: everything disintegrates, recombines, disintegrates…and on and on forever.

Impermanence is an absolute.

As philosophically interesting as that may be, the visceral reality of our eventual, corporeal erasure scares the living crap out of us.

And it is this fear that often negates wisdom.

I realize that these views are not shared by many who have become "true believers": adherents to a "path" devoid of doubt. I wrote much of *"Singing in the Lifeboats"* for the rest of us who are still scratching our heads and wondering what the hell this is all about.

Living without dogmas, doctrines and an instruction manual is really tough.

So what's it going to be?

Resignation or resistance?

We can anesthetize ourselves with the endless circus of dancing clowns who shuck and jive some "'system of salvation"…

or suck it up, stop whining, and embrace our responsibility to perhaps bring some of that *love, justice, mercy, beauty, kindness, and honesty* into this life.

Preachy?

Probably.

But it doesn't make it any less true.

I'm still scribbling.

My Birthday Wish
[a ramble on playing the odds]

Each afternoon, I approach my mailbox with a certain amount of trepidation:

at least two ads for Viagra, "walk-in bathtubs", hearing aids, dental implants, enticing photos of a local retirement village, elevator chairs, hair restorers, orthopedic shoes, AARP, and of course... my favorite: cremation.

At 73 I and can no longer escape the possible relevancy of such "come-ons".

The years are faulty surgeons and their hands shake worse with every year.

But I'm not interested in blunting the "scalpel".

I need the edge of this moment, the exquisite cut and slice of this truth...

so I'm not good at kidding myself.

And *"no"* I don't want *"the extended warrantee"* on this DVD player.

Hell...I'll take my chances...a bet between my aging, genetic blueprint... against some sketchy, Chinese technology with the crappy design and faulty wiring of a mechanism put together by an under paid, over worked wage slave in Beijing.

So for my birthday, all I want is to outlive my gadgets...

Is that asking for much?

The Serpent and the Sunflowers

Somewhere in the deep hum of wind and engines,

a child grew fretful, it's mother quickly quieting its annoyance to a snuffle.

An elderly man requested a pillow from the stewardess, his partner a thin blanket.

Someone's head set was not working properly and the movie was about to begin.

The captain directed their attention to something noteworthy down below.

Breakfast had been served, its detritus cleared away and the talk now was of vacations, both past…

and the one that soon would never be…

for far beneath, in a mind made mad by dogma's venom, a serpent uncoiled and struck…

The villagers reported that bits of bodies rained down on their fields of waving, blooming sunflowers.

White Wine and Raspberries

I'm sitting, frustrated, staring at a white, empty pad of paper…
with nothing coming.

Diane, sensing my irritation, reaches across the table to hand me
one of her juicy, red raspberries. It slips from her hand, landing
in my glass of cold, white wine.

It settles at the bottom like some accidental ruby, clusters of tiny
bubbles clinging to its rosy facets.

"White wine and raspberries"…

"White wine and raspberries"…

Sometimes disparate things come together unexpectedly.

Go ahead and discover some yourself…

maybe even write your own poem about it.

All you have to do is pay attention because such things happen
around you… all the time.

If you get nothing more out of all this…I'm content.

Two Crosses

I saw two wooden crosses draped with fading flowers.

I couldn't read the names...

they were already being erased by sun and rain...

only dark smears ...

Besides, we were going way too fast, our minds and eyes intent on the completion of some special goal.

Over the years I've noticed many such sad monuments on the sides of highways and country roads.

Those who raised these temporary memorials have now gone back to their daily lives where thoughts of death are only the occasional rumblings of a summer storm behind some distant mountain...

nothing more than the fading sizzle of some lightning far, far away.

Besides... it is not advisable to meditate too long on random chance and universal impermanence...

or we would have a glut of poets, artists, and philosophers

who have a habit of making us uncomfortable...

and ruining our "fun."

So the traffic speeds by…

We talk and laugh…

We change the stations and Bluetooth any thought away.

The "Tedsicle"

[a rant on self-delusion]

On July 5, 2002- Ted Williams- formally known as *"The Kid"*, *"The Splendid Splinter"* [really], and *"The Thumper"*- died.

But unlike the usual reports of the demise of such iconic figures… this was just the beginning.

You see Ted- after being separated into head and torso- was frozen at minus 110 degrees in liquid nitrogen by the Alcor Life Extension Foundation.

You'd think that this rather bizarre stab at some future immortality by such a famous figure would be common knowledge…but it isn't.

Go ahead! Ask around.

There is something called *"The Rule of Seven"* that theorizes that generally people have to hear details about something seven times before it penetrates their skulls.

I have my doubts … but just in case, allow me to play along.

Here goes:

1. *Ted's in a deep freeze…like your peas and carrots.*
2. *Ted's not "blowing in the wind" or "pushing up daisies."*
3. *Ted's **not** with Uncle Walt; that's a myth. Do the research.*
4. *Ted's stuck on "third"… indefinitely.*

5. *Ted's got a hefty electricity bill every month.*
6. *Ted's a...well... a "Tedsicle".*
7. *But Ted could have the last laugh.*

Got it now?

Good! Let's move on.

Now if we can manage to really be honest with one another, most of us would admit that we would prefer to hang on to this fleshy package as long as possible...if we're not babbling, wearing a diaper, and drooling.

Old age sucks, no matter what they tell you.

Imagine a new model...maybe with better accessories.

But since we really haven't figured this one out yet, there are countless, compensatory, bogus ways we have devised to escape dealing with our finality.

If you can't afford cryonics...well there's an endless array of old and new tactics of avoidance.

Some usually involve - at the expense of your intelligence- the uncritical acceptance of this or that twaddle: "*You will live forever if you believe [fill in the blank]. Death is just a passage to the next life.*"

Yep...all you need is some faith...not facts...cause facts can be such a buzz kill.

So step right up and escape the ultimate "bummer". It's right here in this sacred book, written by a bunch of sheep herders who were not burdened by science or the inconvenience of...well...facts.

How many millions of people went to their premature graves because of some mono-maniacal, egotistical twat who got them to believe his brand of bull shit?

Sieg Heil!

But if Ted does rise from his icy stasis...complements of his fortune...guess I'll have to re-think that one...but frankly...it's not likely.

All bets are on a future science that will have conquered what are now the insurmountable problems of cell regeneration...critical to our reanimation.

Good luck on that one.

"To be...or not to be"...that really is the question... and we all think we know the answer.

It's obvious; isn't existence preferable to annihilation...to non-existence?

We want to go on forever.

But, each night we fall into that impenetrable darkness.

Where did "I" go?

Where were "I" when "I" returned to consciousness the next morning?

And I returned not only to my body...but to the baggage of my "identities":

those narratives of my life, both past and present that I roll over and over until they become the "pudding" of the "real".

Cheops was buried with a vast retinue of servants, his vital organs preserved in ceremonial jars; going to need'em...especially the "fun" ones...

And Ted's going to belt a few new ones over the wall and then go fishing on week-ends.

When I think of those ransacked pyramids and Cheops' mummified rags and dust being gawked at by Mrs. Brenners's field tripping, fourth grade class, when I imagine old Ted's head swaddled in its icy syrup waiting for a resurrection that I really doubt will ever happen...I think:

"What a failure of the imagination."

Letting go is far harder for some than others, particularly when they've experienced all the best possible advantages that life offers...and they want more...more...more...of the same: sex, money, fame, power, latte's, Italian sport cars, lazy cruises down the Nile... the permutations, the possibilities are ...

well...finite...actually...

You can't get the infinite from finite sums.

How many orgasms to reach infinity?

How long can I sustain this titillation?

Ah... no thanks Ted, Cheops!

If "more" does not stop the annoying commentary of time...

If "more" does not end its desire for it…

If "more" does not brings me home to a place beyond my "self".

I'm not interested.

I came close a few times.

Sweet Melon Melting in my Mouth

Not all sweetness is the same.

Only in August does a melon taste like this.

Other times… only imitations and anemic frauds…

Like so much that we encounter in our lives.

We pay a terrible price for our endless expediencies to satisfy our appetites,

for our impatience,

for the demands of our nagging, petulant desires.

We will not wait.

Not allowed to reach their optimum fruition, they are picked and then transported to the super market down the street.

You can have one in December.

But everything has its time of perfect ripeness.

Clever as we have become…this we cannot force or change.

One bite will tell you that.

Ah…but this melon will have your taste buds singing:

"Ah…sweet melon melting in my mouth…let your sweetness remind me that in order to taste the deeper poetry in all things, sometimes you must have the patience to "ripen" into your own perfection."

Waking Alone

This waking alone is really quite disturbing.

Your absence next to me feels strange, unnerving.

This vacancy, this cold unwrinkled space…

This omission of your form and face…

This missing pillow by my head…

That half unwrinkled side of bed…

The memory of your breathing…

The rolling of your body when you're sleeping…

the warmth that tells me that you're there.

that incremental waking that we share.

How awful this would be

If this were not just temporary

and you weren't gone for just today…

to a town ten miles away.

The Box

Condemned by those who never harbored doubt, Giordano Bruno, a martyr to his inquisitiveness, suffered the flames of Vatican intolerance.

Galileo, forced to recant his heliocentric vision, spent his last nine years muttering *"And yet it's so!"* to himself in an empty room.

You see... "The Faithful"- after punishing the transgressor-lock up all dangerous ideas in a box and seal it with their holy chains, reciting dark incantations of threat and retribution to those who dare espouse them.

Besides, there's just no telling what other "dangers" might be spawned if they were allowed to flutter free.

But it would be a mistake to think that we have come too far to be affected by nonsense and its dogmas...

for somewhere- down below- you can hear faint wings fluttering in the darkness ...

and the rattling of the chains...

while the incense burns, the choir sings, the priest mumbles and the crowd murmurs its acquiescence.

Men with Violins

[a rant on sublimation]

I was checking out the offerings at the local *Red Box* up the street when I noticed a recurrent theme: *"Men with Guns"*...

all kinds of them: big ones, small ones, shiny ones, sinister looking, high capacity magazine ones...

usually in the grip of very pissed off, very muscular, manly men-

although an occasional, equally irate female does find her way into the arsenal.

Why should men have all the fun?

I am not here to comment upon gun ownership and the 2nd Amendment.

I really don't have a particular animus toward guns.

You like guns? Have at it!

As long as you're not a total psycho- and we haven't figured that one out yet- you can collect all the weapons you need for the coming "zombie apocalypse" ...

or whatever catastrophic, L. Ron Hubbard scenario, you have imagined to liven up your otherwise boring and hopelessly dull life.

But this is a tiring narrative, a repetitive motif on billboards, magazines, on advertisements and especially on the inter-net...

and on this *Red Box.*

I gaze about at the people in the store- so many overweight, non -heroic, flabby bodies and those beaten, empty eyes that speak of defeat and resignation.

They move slowly up the aisles of our local Happy Town Cornucopia, their shopping carts filled with things that will surely kill them, or at least give them a case of adult onset diabetes.

They don't come close to the *"Men with Guns"* images I see before me.

Many recognize that this is it!

It's not going to get much better than this.

But when the really "bad guy"- usually a terrorist- gets righteously blown away by the truly "good guy"-the muscular one with lots of guns- each high velocity ejaculation will drain off some of that frustration and deliver a form of subliminal, compensatory release- that like any addictive drug- will be needed the next time the pressure mounts.

Like porno, it's only momentarily satisfactory, and that's the whole point.

You'll keep coming back and this Red Box will have new heroes with bigger guns…

until maybe someday, fantasy is insufficient, and we hear about that psycho in the theater, or the monster in that school.

The solution: *"If only everyone had been armed…"*

I am weary of this unrelenting redundancy, by the repetition of a point of view that maintains the brutal context from which we cannot seem to escape.

I am angered by the incessant manipulation of our fears and discontents, of the constant pulling on the "trigger" of pseudo assuagements that profit others.

I am waiting for "*Men with Violins*".

The Familiarity of Things

That spoon, that knife, that platter that you use for your spaghetti-

How many meals, how many years have consecrated these simple things so that now they are filled with such meaning they tears sometimes come to me whenever I begin to wash them?

This is the way with all the simple objects of our lives, all the pots and pans, the hammers, all the things we mistakenly brand as "trivial".

All objects become imbued with history and meaning...

the passage of our lives, the fleeting meals and moments, the pleasure and yes, sometimes the pain when sadness was served on that now chipped and broken platter.

The feel and heft of things grow with the marriage of our hands until they become old friends and bring to us the comfort of the familiarity of things...in this harsh, uncaring universe.

Killer Chickens

[a rant on the wonders of science]

It's all over the Internet. A dentist from Minnesota killed a much beloved and treasured icon of the African tourist traffic: a majestic lion.

Photographed by thousands, the "Lion King" was now reduced to buzzard bait and a stuffed trophy head on this dental dimwit's study wall.

I guess asserting his expertise through braces, root canals and dentures were insufficient proof of his penile prowess....so...it was off to the Dark Continent to plug a testimony to his macho virility.

It was stressed that he first shot the lion with a bow and then tracked him for 40 hours – the poor lion bleeding and in agony from the embedded arrow.

He finally administered the coup de grace with a high-powered hunting rifle...from a safe distance...

A heinous act, according to the worldwide internet, but so went the Buffalo, Passenger Pigeon, and the infamous Dodo Bird.

The news is still out on the Loch Ness lizard.

It's not news though; we're really, really good at killing shit.

So maybe all we can do is to even the odds a bit.

Many of us have read those weird, Frankenstein stories of the grafting of frog genes to vegetables or cereal grains infused with wasp sperm...don't ask...

But what if – through the wonders of further genetic manipulation – they manage to graft a Lion's genes to a chicken's for the purpose of producing larger, meatier drumsticks and breasts...but it all sort of back fires with unintended consequences.

These chickens are bigger and very aggressive.

Thanks to the wonders of science...they're predators...with the requisite attitude.

They travel from town to town leaving total devastation in their wake.

Did I mention they were carnivorous?

These are not Perdue chickens.

No more the need to travel far away to expensive, exotic hunting grounds.

"Oh -that one? Well I bagged it when I was going out to the backyard to empty the trash!"

Spoonfuls

I remember them when I would visit my mother in the nursing home.

They were always in that same corner.

I remember the patient, careful offerings of that spoon, his palsied hand shaking slightly as he fed his equally aged wife who gazed off into some distant past- when hand-in-hand- they walked the warm beaches of their youth and sipped sweet wine from their crystal glasses.

Now it has all come down to this.

In the midst of all our schemes, we are caught off guard by the incursions of time …

until we reach this place for the last spoonfuls of love…

if we're lucky!

The Last Two Words

A sign in front of a church as we drive by:

"See others as God sees you."

Diane did some editing:

"Leave off the last two words".

I aspire to such eloquent brevity.

Snowman Melting in the Rain

He's melting ...a casualty of the rain and the rising temperature.

He sports a black olive nose and one carrot eye, the other already on the ground.

You made him while taking a break from clearing a path to the dog kennel.

Now a light rain is whittling him away still more, but he remains standing in dissolving, obstinate defiance.

I like the purple scarf.

In the end, it's all about managing a bit of panache.

With a sagging, pale blue hat and a piece of crooked tinfoil for a smile, he's losing his shape and substance.

I can relate.

I don't know what I was doing while you were working your artistry in this white medium of impermanence, but again...I missed out.

I should have been out there with you...a long time ago...

one more snowman melting in the rain.

"Weltschmerz?"

[A Rant for Whiners]

[Weltschmerz: German for "world weariness"…that feeling of sadness you get when you consider the enormous suffering caused by the overwhelming number of jerks, assholes, murderers, and general morons who populate this planet at any given moment.]

Recently, in a casual coffee house conversation, I learned that they now have dogs capable of much more than guiding the blind.

Some are now trained to detect the subtle signs of seizures and mood swings.

Then they alert you so you can take your meds.

I thought that that was very cool.

I like that…a whole lot better than those dogs in the airports with their hyper olfactory senses who cause you to wind up splayed on a wall wailing like a little girl: *"Honestly, I don't know how that got there!"*

Yeah, what we really need in this era of general malaise are canines who can detect our sagging spirits, or what our German brethren have labeled as "Weltschmertz" –

[See above.]

- A particularly ironic expression, when you consider the amount of death and destruction that country has contributed to the 20th century.

But I digress.

Here's how it goes: at the first signs of a minute change in your breathing pattern, perhaps some barely perceptible chemical sign of incipient depression, maybe a subtle drooping of your shoulders, a despairing tone in your voice, your dyspeptic flatulence, your flagging libido-[Don't ask!]

they immediately go into action: -dancing on their hind legs, rolling their eyes and flailing their tongues while howling Beethoven's *Ode to Joy*...

anything to halt your precipitous descent into the sink hole of existential dread...

anything to stop you from resorting to Sartre and Camus or studying Brueghel and Bosch's visions of hell while listening to Kurt Cobain on your I-phone...

So here's some helpful advice:

Avoid those annoying, yippy "rat dogs" that people living in trailer parks tend to have. When they're not whiny little bitches, they're mounting someone's leg. They've got their own issues and can't help you.

Poodles wouldn't work because they are genetically programmed to go for the Brie and a nice bottle of Burgundy at the first signs of "ennui" or anything less than 'joi de vivre"; they could care less about your emotional "contretemps".

I'd really avoid Dobermans and Pit Bulls; they also won't give a crap about your "Weltschmerz" ...but they will tear out your throat to shut you the hell up, you spine-less weakling!

Stay away from "petting whores"; you know…the ones who can't wait to throw themselves on their backs for a cheap belly rub. What happened the last time you fell for that while drunk and stupid?

Those butt- ugly, goofy looking ones, [I have no idea how to spell their names] with all that loose, wrinkled skin also probably would not do the job. The first time they see a picture of Rin-Tin-Tin…they'll succumb to the canine version of "Weltschmerz" and just lay around in profound resignation, too depressed to even lick their balls, realizing that they only way they'll ever get laid is to hump the closest leg…yours!

German shepherds– with their superior intelligence, exemplary Nordic profiles, and Aryan purity -not to mention their perfect guard dog demeanors-would be best.

Besides, you need a little "tough love", you pathetic, self-pitying, little sniveler!

Glad I could help!

[For further information; see "Canines for Comfort" on our YouTube page.]

Raining Catalpa Blossoms

It's the end of July, the time of raining Catalpa blossoms.

The ancient, towering tree that has shaded our cars and tarmac is shedding its bouquets of perfume clusters…

raining down like a scene in a Kurosawa film where two samurai face off in a duel held within some pink blizzard of floating cherry blossoms.

Sometimes we stand beneath it, looking through its swaying, defoliating boughs at the blue sky and passing clouds.

I smell vanilla with a touch of sweet gardenia.

You may experience something completely different.

That's the thing about Catalpas: they lend themselves to individual interpretation.

But like all beauty, the price is often hefty.

Now those blossoms must be rapidly removed before the heat of the summer sun bakes and burns them into a pungent, sticky brown paste that stains everything.

As we drive off each morning, we leave behind a cloud of their milky petals, like some spontaneous float in some impromptu parade.

So if you ever have the chance - go stand in a rain of Catalpa blossoms.

You'll walk away the poet you have always been…

but were too fearful to become.

Being the Captain
[a rant on the Dharma]

Lately, more evidence of our less than unique status in this cosmos seems to be coming in on a daily basis. As always, it's all about context; and in the context of the solar system, we are not very special. There are hundreds of millions of other solar systems, so maybe we should get a grip on our overblown sense of exceptionalism.

We are a tiny dust particle floating around in a cloud of planets and forces we will probably never truly understand. Astronomers-after examining a relatively tiny slice of the cosmos- have reported thousands of planets that could support life.

So, the question does arise: who is in charge of all this? The idea of some kind of "Cosmic Captain" is becoming increasingly suspicious. Our ship is floating in this immense ocean and he is nowhere to be found ... and judging from history and in the daily news reports – appears to be periodically insane... or insanely drunk.

The Buddhists refer to this situation as the "*Dharma*" – the realization of the way things actually are, once we have ceased our projections born of fear and desire.

The urge to believe anything that alleviates our doubts and our fears is as powerful as our instinct to survive. In fact... they are connected... or so we think.

We are adrift, but refuse to accept the helm. We want something/ someone else – real or imaginary – to take control, to take responsibility, to tell us what to believe ... how to be.

The task of discovering our way through our own acts of imagination and creativity seems overly daunting...

So the first smug, shifty bastard with a gift of gab and a bag of promises catches our attention and we too join the legions of the "true believers" as we row away toward some foggy, promised Elysium where our fears will be removed and are vague desires finally realized.

We need to stop being mindless galley slaves rowing for others.

Near Miss

A poem can arrive from the most unlikely place.

I just heard –that on its way from deep, dark outer space-

a comet's coming that will pass real close and barely miss us,

but relax- there's no need now to make a fuss.

Cause this won't happen until the year 2036 –

and for me - it's close but thankfully- a near miss.

But wait a minute – that would make me 93 –

Hardly likely – but still – a possibility.

And I know by then I'd have so many mixed emotions;

I'd be leaning on a walker, swallowing a hundred pills and potions.

And it must be mighty lonely near the end

when you've lost your hair, your libido, and all your friends.

So I am quite thankful for another great excuse

To indulge in all my favorite forms of self abuse.

Cause, if it's not some stupid, God- damned comet,

There's something else with your name upon it.

So kick it back and take nothing very seriously.

Why cause yourself unnecessary misery.

I know it sounds like some trite "cliché",

too pedestrian for me to say...

but -I'm going to say it anyway:

The problem's not dying-it's living.

Our Stories

This backyard leviathan towers above us.

and I know the incident behind this all quite well:

how- unintentionally- you once mowed it down...

leaving it a struggling wisp of pine, reduced to ragged stubble.

how- near bye, a ripped, Tibetan prayer flag tied to a rusting twelve foot pole snapped and jerked its ancient Buddhist sutras of healing and compassion into the surrounding air.

how... I imagined- that through those first hard years-the injured pine listened very closely.

At first it felt a mild tingling in the remnants of its fragile roots and a surge returned to send new growth into the close embrace of air and sun.

Today, the light- through its snow bent boughs- creates a yellow, bright corona, while a sudden gust of freezing wind sends a small avalanche down upon us

You told me all about this when we first started this journey together.

Forty years have passed.

Now I think about it every time I work outside, occasionally pausing to marvel at its girth and height.

When I stop- because my back and breath are not what they use to be- I look up into its lofty branches and think about all this.

Cow Farts

[a ramble on gas]

Yes folks, the numbers are in: the methane levels are rising: everywhere, everything is sinking into the melting permafrost.

Polar bears are drowning.

Skin cancers are soaring...

Forests are being devoured by beetles who love this new climate.

World heat indexes are climbing to record highs.

Most island nations are already moving out as their beaches disappear.

In short: we're screwed!

And all while we chow down on another Big Mac, barbecue those ribs, and throw another hot dog on the grill to the accompanying score of bovine flatulence.

Perhaps it's no accident that the reported cattle mutilations always include cored out anuses.

Maybe the same thing happened on their bleak, dead, desiccated planet before they retired down below.

Come to think of it, many humans have reported some rather invasive probes as part of their unsolicited, annual physical.

Whatever the reasons, they – whoever "they" might be- are very interested in our nether regions, the last conduits of our insatiable appetites.

If they have conquered the unimaginable distances in space travel, it is not too far- fetched to wonder if they have not also defeated the most formidable of enemies: Time.

And they know what we're in for…but they cannot intervene… because they've picked up episodes of *"Star Trek"* …

and the Prime Directive forbids any interference with the development…or destruction of any alien civilizations.

That was forbidden by *"The Kirk"*.

As for us: done in by cow farts and the platitudes of a hack.

Swimming through Entropy.
[a ramble on futile tactics]

"Entropy: things tend to progress from order to disorder." [Translation-Your shit falls apart.]

Lately, we've been getting a selection of glossy, un- solicited magazines. Whether it's a prank or some accident of demographics, I'll never know.

One of these magazines is *"Ebony"*, the other *"The Economist"*.

I keep telling the publishers to stop sending them but they keep coming.

It's all pretty ironic because I am a 73 year old white man with little or no economic acumen.

But I've learned of special creams conducive to maintaining my velvety, lush and dark complexion…

And I have to tell you that I'm groovin' and movin' like Sammy Davis.

But I still can't balance my checkbook.

I've been doing "Voodoo check balancing" for years.

But thanks to *"The Economist"*, I've learned clever strategies for bloating my portfolio beyond any greedy expectations and I am now a sophisticate, a veritable linguist in the turgid, economic vocabulary of the "Masters of Wall Street."

Junk bonds anyone?

But in the end, it all comes down to just more futile tactics for swimming through this "sea of entropy" and attempting to escape those sharks that always seem to be so close behind and gaining.

Black or white, rich or poor...it's all the same to them.

Making Pizzelles
[a ramble on last things]

Each year -at Christmas- Diane makes pizzelles, those traditional Italian cookies- redolent with Anise, circular, thin, light.

I can't help but think of that Eucharist wafer the Priest use to give us … before I began to suspect something. It will stick to the roof of your mouth the same way though, if you wait too long.

Basho use to wait for the fragments that occasionally fell to the floor…not by accident of course.

He's gone and the emptiness is profound.

These moments are now significant, significant in the way we endow such things with the sadness that only comes with our awakening to impermanence.

I believe we need to allow ourselves to feel this sadness born of our awareness that we have entered the realm of "last things".

Before they even ask me, I tell them that I am not interested in buying extra time insurance on my purchase. Five extra years seems overly optimistic… and I see no reason to attract attention to whatever unknown forces have had a bad day and want to ruin mine…sometime…in the near future…before the five years run out.

From observing our fading garden to the floral spirals of distant galaxies …we begin to "get it".

So here I sit, watching Diane make pizzelles –without old Basho-watching each movement of her hands as she drops a dollop of dough on to that special iron that stamps each one with an ornamental design.

I see the small spiral of steam that escapes each time and hear its muffled hiss.

It's like that Japanese tea ceremony, where every movement, every gesture, is calculated to keep you present.

She performs this ritual with a practiced grace, timing each one to its aromatic perfection.

And I am reminded by Basho's absence that these pizzelles…could be my last ones.

Mother Night

The storm came and smothered our house with its wings of white stillness.

It blew out our lights, sent us in fumbling in search of batteries and candles,

had us ripping and rolling all the old news into tight logs to ignite our old, iron stove.

We shared a meal, laughed at the erupting howls of wind that made us wince at the tree limb scrapping the roof.

How close the past remains, only the fragile membrane of our technology separating us from Mother Night... who sleeps so deep in the matrix of our neurons, bones and flesh.

She is never far, her black wings invisible until some break in that tenuous divide reminds us that she is always waiting, ready to embrace us, to remind us of our journey...to remind us of all our gains...and losses.

We have sacrificed much on the altars of our clever gadgetry.

Once we huddled together for safety, warmth and comfort, telling our stories, our fanciful myths of the mysteries all around us.

When a faint rustle or the distant roar of some terrible dark thing broke in to startle us awake from dreaming, we drew together, feeling comfort in our numbers.

Now, when the lights surge back, when we hear our machines wake from their mechanical slumbers, our eyes will recoil from the sudden shock of that jarring luminescence.

We had grown accustomed to the gentle, flickering dance of flames and shadows.

Atlantis Redux 2.0
[a ramble on consequences]

I watched a short video on what the world would look like if most of the ice melted.

And according to the experts, it's not "*if*", but "*when*".

My first reaction was: "*We're really screwed.*"

It seems the sea level would increase by 216 feet.

Maybe that's extreme, but even a 100 feet would do the job.

And seeing as we are only ten miles from the coast, I think it's fair to say that we are not in the "safe zone".

I've heard that they are now sweating the implications of a 6 foot rise by the end of this century.

I wandered around our yard, imagining schools of multi- colored, phosphorescent fish swimming around the remains of our trees, through our garden, over our lawn and our submerged, crumbling house.

I turned back to stare at the weather worn Buddha still sitting in profound meditation in our garden.

The crinkle on his lips seemed to say: "*All just more of the same brother: the rise and fall of seas, mountains, and empires- bobbing in and out on the tides of time.*"

We live in such a short sliver of all this; it's not easy to take the long view.

But I realized there was a better than good chance that few of us now will be around for the real drama.

I went back inside. I needed the assuagement of the "familiar".

The radio began to report some of the daily awfulness that we hear so often.

We no longer even shake our heads in horror and disbelief.

Maybe we really do need this "rebooting" to finally allow the consequences of our greed, ignorance, and animosities to change our hearts.

The daily slaughter and ruin are reported in the same tone as the weather report and the sports.

We are running out of time on this version, and the continued creeping up of the water level will be a barometer of the compassion and love that we were not been able to muster for this wondrous earth...

and one another.

Basho

Today we brought you home in a simple, wooden box.

I held it in my hand, surprised at its lightness.

You were a big dog- over 115 lbs...and now this.

Memories flooded me ...

All those rides in our old VW bus, you perched on the back seat

with the wind rustling your brindled fur, your big head resting on the arm rest.

You were in that quiet space that only Akitas can enter.

All those walks around the cranberry bog and the lake around the corner...

walks that grew increasingly shorter as we both got older.

All those belly-up times in the kitchen as Diane prepared dinner... or those special

moments when she sat at her stool making those great smelling, Italian cookies,

occasionally dropping the crumbs that you waited for with such patience.

You were our samurai protector.

When you barked, we paid attention because you never indulged in anything gratuitous.

Those first, early, winter days when we let you run in the fenced garden, your black, puppy nose

suddenly erupting from the newly fallen snow, your infectious exuberance making us laugh along

with your unbridled joy.

To be greeted each time … as it were the first.

and now… all …all…in a box?

Lead Buddha

"The trick is to squeeze out as much of the water as possible." '[Diane]

This takes time…no shortcuts.

You've placed a heavy lead Buddha on a small board placed across the deep purple eggplant that you've sliced and spread out on your cutting board.

And there will be no "time saving" opening of a jar.

Yes, there is a reason the old boy is smiling, his arms raised in a joyous gesture of celebration.

I swear I can see his lead belly quivering slightly in anticipation.

I know…a stupid projection…but that's the way I see and feel it every time you prepare this treat.

Stand in that kitchen and smell the simmering herbs, garlic, wine, tomato, the unique pungency of the cooking eggplant…all blending with the melting, imported parmesan.

No corners are cut. This is it…right now…no other "now"… but "now"…and each "now" is not a mere stepping stone to the next.

That is the way I want to greet each fleeting day, my arms raised in praise and anticipation…

to become so lead heavy that I sink into each moment with a joyous presence…

to treasure the details, knowing that this is the practice, the Dharma of being present in the only time we have...

to love the simple things in and for themselves...

to slow down and do it right...

this moment, this breath, this movement of hand and mind... together...

all to squeeze out what does not contribute to the final Dharma of a well lived life...

and damn great eggplant parmesan.

It's for you
[a ramble on progress]

Hundreds of saffron monks, droning their ancient prayers- waited for the official announcement.

Yeshi Norbu, his Holiness, the 14th Dalai Lama was leaving his body.

The muffled rustling of their prayer beads and soft chanting filled the air in the court yard...

all to help his passage through the Bardo Thodol- that passage from death to liberation.

Even such an evolved soul needs the space when the breath of body ceases and the flight of spirit begans.

We need time to free our "selves" from the imprints, the shackles of all desires, a practice never too soon begun.

Usually, we wait until the pulls of passion and hunger ebb

and the subsequent diminution of desire begins.

For most this period of transition is long and the demons many as we unravel the knots of lust and suffering we have caused ourselves...and others.

It would not be long this time.

He had consulted with Western shamans, those scientists and physicists who use a mathematical language as complex and precise as the Sanskrit used in their ancient texts, both traditions concerned with the very nature of the void in which the spinning cycles of birth and death conduct their eternal dance.

His Holiness had announced- after long and profound thought and meditation- that they must find a new way, a better way, a less vulnerable way than the usual corporeal re-generation- to convey the great Truths that would free all from the recurrent nightmares of this world.

His Holiness had upset the Tibetan Diaspora of forced exiles and those still bound in their own land by announcing that he would not re-incarnate in the flesh as those before him had done for millennia.

There would not be the usual searching and testing of young boys that followed the passing of each Anointed One.

As usual, compassion was the point of it all…but survival was contingent on adaptation.

Abbots Tashi Dhargey and Palden Schubu- sat beside His Holiness, hanging on each slow and fragile breath, their voices quietly intoning the same prayer as the waiting monks outside.

Finally- a silence deeper than any they had ever achieved through their own meditations filled the room.

His Holiness had told Abbot Dhargey-whose name suggested progress- that he would communicate in a new way… directly with him when the last vestiges of this last incarnation had fallen from his spirit like the dew from a waking Lion's mane.

The Abbot, confused and at a loss due to the uncertainty that His Holiness' announcement had caused him, walked from the room into the blazing, Indian noon day sun, searching his mind for the proper words... when the incongruous ring of a cell phone from one of the seated monks broke the reverential silence like a crashing tea cup in a sacred ceremony...

And young Choden Dorje- who had crossed the guarded borders into this refuge - vaulted to his feet, his eyes weeping tears of joy, his voice choking with excitement - announcing -as he handed his phone to Abbot Dhargey: *"It's for you!"*

Solitary, self-absorbed Sweaty Meditation"
[a ramble on obsession]

"If you can read this- Your second."

That's what it said on the big guys red tank top in shouting stark, white letters.

It's a visual thing – you had to see it.

He was busy moving huge chunks of steel... up and down... up and down in the solitary, repetitive choreography of weightlifters.

Formulaic pop music oozed over the entire scene like some sugared melt of banal adrenaline and the vulgar obvious. A wall of Televisions tuned to different stations bathed the whole scene in a wash of morphing colors.

And the faces... on the TV... so perfect... so symmetrical, veritable algorithms of balance and harmony...

and the bodies...also perfect... Soap Opera Apollos and Cosmetic Aphrodites...

unlike the scene below...but they were trying.

Old tired men who knew that their girth could kill them, monitored their pulses with visible trepidation while svelte, young fauns, attempting to make themselves worthy of an ad for lip gloss, evaluated themselves in the hand smudged, foggy mirrors.

These were the good years… before the pounds started creeping back.

Meanwhile, the big guy was working hard, huffing and puffing like some 19th-century steamroller…all while casting admiring glances at his reflections.

And all around, the harsh clanks and clangs went off in a random firing order and the futile battle against the dissolution of the flesh raged on…

while "your" deep into your solitary, self absorbed, sweaty meditation.

Confetti Parade

We followed a truck the other day piled high with October leaves.

They hadn't been covered so we watched as the leaves made their spinning escape, swirling into the air…like old, crinkly, dry confetti.

It was a bit mesmerizing, watching those leaves annotate our slow parade.

We had to wonder if this was not all intentional, the natural attrition of wind plus speed, negating any necessity for them to be dumped somewhere.

The harsh, raw air made me think of the winter that waited ahead.

For me, the worst part was the natural dwindling of the light that creates a shifting collage of shadows, a grayness that triggers my inherent melancholy.

Once- it took me to the ancient, colonial cemetery down the street where I wandered among the crumbling head stones, attempting to piece together some narrative from the dates and names of people who lived in this town a few centuries before…a few perhaps in our house.

Its rusted, hanging gate, reminded me of those old Lon Chaney and Bella Lugosi films that played each Saturday night on "*Creature Feature*"; I could almost hear the creepy, cheesy, Theremin music announcing the arrival of Count Dracula or the Wolf Man. I loved those old black and white movies.

Some of the stones were totally shattered from their bases, lying in busted, ragged fragments. Our park workers are respectful of them and attempt to maintain some jig saw integrity by piecing what they can on the ground. Many stones lean at precarious angles, soon to join their fallen neighbors.

It's a particularly gloomy scene when a light snow has fallen and the meager light of our short, New England days cast shadows on the stones around them.

I feel like a 3rd rate Edgar Allan Poe.

That's when the memory of this day- our laughter, a slow truck, the spastic vertigos of leaves, their soft whisperings as they swirl away- will be a balance to such melodrama.

It's never too early to start collecting for those nights when you start to forget that it's all just a crazy parade with confetti leaves escaping into the cooling air.

Another Cliché Castle

I had a dream of sand castles on a cliché beach under a cliché sun.

It was like every beach on every postcard I'd ever seen on tourist kiosks everywhere.

Great… even my sub-conscious was an unimaginative hack.

This was the best it could come up with?

But then it got more interesting.

Most of the castles were the usual: childish constructions by pail and shovel-but a few were ornate structures, complex with soaring filigrees of towers that spoke of more mature, loftier architectural skills.

I realized that they represented where I had been, where I was now…and where I hoped to be.

But now it's 6:30 in the morning and I'm sitting in this kitchen sipping a cooling cup of coffee, waiting, wanting to write something…something really worthy.

Then I realized that once I built sand castles for the simple joy of it…

…and I began to write.

Suitable for Cubicles
[a rant on when it's enough]

There was a vague dullness in their eyes.

It was a void, a flattening out of all the irregularities and incongruities that individuals usually exhibit...

until they run the gauntlet of schools and culture.

Ok... ok...it wasn't all of them...but for me...after almost forty years...

there were too many.

This never ceased to shock me, no matter how many times I witnessed it and attempted to pierce through their learned dullness.

Now I've heard all the repeated, excusatory bromides that *"if you can just reach a couple... blah, blah, blah."*

I'm not going to dispute the truth or the obvious benefit for adopting such an attitude, especially when you're just beginning your career...

but after forty years... it was enough; you can keep the self-serving platitudes.

Conversation with most of them was like-employing a scatological metaphor- attempting to extract a boulder from an elephant's ass.

And I tried but it seemed that any extended interaction with them was becoming more difficult.

Was I getting that old?

Perhaps… but something had changed and it was not for the better.

They would be sitting in the darkness of the classroom, already transfixed by their flashing screens, their faces reflecting the shimmer and fluidity of the quickly changing scenes.

I realized that they no longer even spoke to one another.

No one had thought to turn on the lights.

I mean…imagine a pitch black room with cell phone and computer lights reflecting off their transfixed faces.

"Creepy" hardly describes it.

On the last day of class, I would ask them to write the name of just one of their classmates nearest to them, their neighbors for four months.

Few knew… even when I bribed them with extra credit.

Most of them had to be made suitable for cubicles, for functions of the digital age that did not require original thought, much less creativity.

Only a few would steer the helm of this *"Brave New World."*

The first thing that had to go was the capacity for ecstasy.

Joy tends to bring about a realization that much of what you've been taught is totally, self serving bullshit.

Next... wonder has to be manipulated and directed because we need you interested in what we need you interested in...like those screens.

A common thought of too many students was a shared, utilitarian philosophy that stated:

"It has to be functional, useful, practical... if it isn't...well that's why we have art and English majors."

On occasion I spoke of my fears for where all this was going. I'd learned to entertain myself.

It was like addressing a herd of legless bison about my fear of their flagging mobility.

Always the idealistic fool, I occasionally dared to speak of *love, beauty, transcendence, truth, justice, compassion.*

When I felt truly brave, I even read them a few lines of poetry...

in between the rules of rhetoric.

They would stare at me with a confusion that morphed into resentment.

"What the fuck is this? This isn't a poetry course... Don't understand that shit anyway!

and...

What in the hell is he going on about anyway?

and…

Is this gonna to be on the test cause it's not in the syllabus?"

and…

And that was when I left.

Down Below

[a ramble on history]

Today, I went down below into our dirt cellar; it's really more of a cellar hole.

Our house is centuries old, so we won't be putting in a bar and a pool- for the spiders- anytime soon.

Besides serving as a very modest wine cellar, it's a depository for all the detritus of our lives, my mother's mostly.

I began to organize things into different boxes.

One was for the throw away stuff, another for what was going to the Salvation Army, and the last...

well... stuff I didn't know what to do with.

Most of what was stored was from my mother's former house in California.

She died a few years ago and I stored a lot of her pictures, and household items... down below.

This was no easy task...especially the photographs.

It's hard to discard any picture, even of a stranger.

They hadn't been strangers to my mother.

The "?" box began to overflow.

Now at 73 everything is a reminder of the fragility and brevity of this life.

I am melancholic by nature and this task just reinforced it.

I found a really old photo of myself, sporting a childish tangle of blond curls and a sly grin.

It reminded me of when- possessed by a nascent sensuality- I took off all my clothes and ran naked through the garden and orchard of the old couple who took care of me in the French countryside after the war. My mother sent me out of Paris because food was easier to get ...and she was an attractive widow and was being courted by an American G.I who eventually came in a big black car and whisked us all away to the States...

and now I'm writing this with no clue of where it will take me.

I thought back to that day in that orchard: the sun on my bare skin, the ripening grapes thick above me, their deep purple, their sweet taste...

all the bees settling on the fallen fruit at my bare feet...really had to watch my step...

and dozens of beds of white and yellow lilies with a hundred wands of gladiolas by an ancient stone wall waving in the breeze ... all the bouquet flowers that the old couple grew to sell in the Parisian market places every week-end...

The aroma of those blue and white lilacs as breezes painted the whole scene with their animated colors...

and me… in the middle of all that …crouching naked in the noon day sun…

That's what often happens when you dwell on the remnants of the past that reside way down below.

That day…I threw away no pictures.

A New Kind of Zombie

Not the slavering, lurching, moaning, cannibalistic ones…

No…I'm thinking of a new kind of zombie.

These zombies would return with an insatiable appetite for the missed opportunities of their former lives.

When they breathed their last, they would awaken in a place of shadows and drifting mists…

not unlike the "Bardos" reported by the Tibetans.

They would stumble about- like they had in life-chasing phantom lights, attempting to discern vague whispers…voices familiar… yet too muddled to be understood.

Eventually they would find themselves back among us, invisible, inanimate and glassy eyed, standing still on our street corners, in our rooms everywhere, in dark corners and bright places…

crying softly…with a pain so palpable that their inaudible weeping would make us wonder what was disturbing the surrounding air:

Memories of rejected love…

Possibilities…for which they were not there…

while they pursued some illusion of fulfillment.

All the beauty, compassion, kindness, friendship, and warmth…

to which they remained oblivious…or ignored…

would now be clear and unimaginably painful.

And they would try to tell us that once they were like us.

Islands of Momentary Light

Many will tell you that they can see the main land…

It's just up ahead… Just follow their directions.

It's true: it's not easy to keep sailing through these shrouded waters with no clear destination.

That's why we are often tricked by those whose mouths drip with the eloquence of their certitudes, whose eyes flare with their extravagant visions.

But a choice has to be made.

We have to do more than just bob around on the swells of our doubts and indecisions.

But some decisions can prove so difficult…especially when you tend toward the "abstract" more than the tangible.

Everywhere, the products of sweat and muscle are evidence of the "real"…

What are "words" compared to the breadth of walls and the reach of sky scrapers?

I lay no bricks and move no rocks …

just these words you're reading now.

You see- only a few of us can manage to admit how "lost" we truly are.

Our compass needle moves in every direction.

But there is one voyage that we all know:

we sail out from darkness… and then back,

our voyages occasionally interrupted by brief respites on the islands of momentary light where we share our poems…

like I'm doing now.

Fools and fakes will tell you they know more.

Amontillado and Redemption
[a ramble on free associations]

I was on my way to replenish my empty wine cellar- a euphemism for a small, dusty wooden rack in our colonial, cob webbed, dry dirt cellar.

Every time I go down those creaking, narrow steps it always reminds me of that Poe story- *"The Cask of Amontillado".*

You know it; we all read it in high school.

The story where Montresor – an affronted, arrogant nobleman-lures a drunken Fortunato into his wine cellar with the promise of sharing a bottle of his rare sherry…and then commences to shackle the poor son-of-a-bitch to the wall and brick him up alive, probably one of the worst cases of over-reaction ever imagined.

No one knows what the poor bastard did to deserve such a horrible fate, but we all know that some people just cannot take a joke.

Fortunato is drunk, but Montressor is really nuts.

That's how- on my way to buy some wine - all this came together. Why? I have no idea…but that's the way it rolls sometimes; I am powerless against it.

Then I was again derailed by a sign on a side door before the entrance to the store:

"Enter here for Redemption."

Immediately my mind went "theological". It was just too tempting.

"*Redemption*" is a pretty heavy word.

But the truth is: I didn't feel the slightest need for "*redemption*".

I'm certainly not a candidate for canonization. I've kicked up some dirt and thrashed about a bit, I admit.

But all I have in my actual cellar is this crummy wine rack…

and in my metaphoric one, no moldering, mummifying corpse entombed in the walls of my vanity and umbrage.

This was a door for Montressor, not me.

I recommend sharing a nice bottle of "*Amontillado*"…anything… and leaving the chains and bricks to others.

A Damn Good Thing

Sometimes I sit at the kitchen table, drinking coffee, and I think about what I really know for sure.

It's a very short list.

I've lived over 73 years… and I'm still confused.

Everywhere I hear voices speaking in the authoritarian tone of those in the "know".

I envy their confidence, their sense of self-possession.

But I can't help but wonder about how much of it is "real"…and how much of it is a product of our ability to anesthetize ourselves from the pangs of doubt through the self-hypnosis of our invented "certitudes"?

I'll never answer that one…or be a convert…

never.

But when my life seems like nothing more than a rotting drift of failures…

when I view the empty husks of my foolish desires and preoccupations…

when I find myself wallowing in despair and regret…

You walk into the kitchen…

And I think : at least I knew a damn good thing when I saw it.

Trivial Background Conversations
[a ramble on being an "extra"]

You know… that scene in almost every movie when the lead actors are reciting their important lines while in the background- always in a public place – a restaurant, maybe-there are tables of "extras" in animated conversations.

You can't make out a word, but you can see they're smiling and the gesticulations of their hands and mouths create a context for the real drama that's unfolding. Have you ever wondered about what they're actually saying to one another? Maybe nasty things or wise cracks about the "stars":

"She's had her face lifted so many times, the only expression she's got left is "hunh?""

or…

"Getting a little 'mucho in the paunch-o amigo. Better cut back on the burritos."

or…

"That slut's seen more action than the Holland Tunnel."

Bitterness is always an option, especially with clever people; and when we realize that this might be as good as it gets: endless bit parts, commercials, and worst of all-summer stock.

It's not that all of them were better than you; they weren't.

But the accidental concatenation of genes and circumstances often trumps talent.

The harsh reality is that most of us are scripted to be "extras", for trivial, background conversations. Just because our Little Red Engine has been *"Yes, I canning…yes I canning"* - up "impossible hill"- does not obligate the universe to show us mercy or its largesse.

So while we have the chance, let's ignore the ignominy of the scripts that we've been handed and refrain from the disappointment that reduces us to the trivialities of bitterness and anger.

We are not superfluous addendums to our lives.

While in the background, let's recite our poems, sing our songs, share roses from our gardens and aromatic dishes from our kitchens.

The Way Things Are

[a rant /poem on acceptance]

Eventually, you have to accept *the way things are*. I realize that in America, this is hard to do.

This is the land of infinite possibilities and choices: face lifts, tummy tucks, and daily discoveries that will keep you goin' long and strong…until that rubber band inside you finally snaps and the friction wheels stop spinning.

We hunger for some special, magic rare elixir, an ointment of palliation…some wizard's potion that will aid us in the avoidance of life's inherent suffering.

The Greeks had a word for it: *"Nepenthe"*- an ancient drug that induced forgetfulness of sadness and trouble. Of course we have developed our own variations on this theme.

Ask your doctor.

Change the channel.

Have another one!

We love any propaganda that reinforces our faith in an infinite variety of "stuff" that will lead us to some incremental, vague salvation.

We have transformed the earth into a glut of luxuries and dalliances: 100 brands of cereal, two hundred stations of distractions, exercises and new diets, new ways to achieve multiple, tumultuous orgasms, celebrities and demigods, old and new religions that promise permutations of immortality… anything to escape… *the way things are.*

You've managed to gather fancy, framed proofs of your authority …while others cannot even scratch their names in the dirt outside their hovels.

You're basking by your marble pool while others bend in the brutal sun, picking with their calloused hands, what you will have for dinner with your friends tomorrow night.

That's just … *the way things are.*

But Time has a way of blurring all sharp delineations, lines fading and drifting, wandering off on tangents of their own.

Look in the mirror.

It's always so much more than we imagined or expected.

We wind up befuddled.

Too many of the promising become the smelly old men who entrap you in endless, addled, one way conversations.

Yesterday you ran the cool, gold, empty beach at dawn, the wind at your back, the rising warmth on your face, your perfect body glistening like pink glass, the gulls circling, cawing above…

and you were thinking: *"How wonderful it all is"*…

And it was…until…

Something "zigged" instead of "zagged" and now it's all scary ambiguity and chance that even Einstein would not accept…

because God is no cheap hustler and does not cast the dice.

But the "dice" keep rolling...

Sometimes it's lucky sevens... sometimes cold eyed snakes.

Sometimes ... we sing like angels...sometimes we howl like beasts...

and that's *the way things really are.*

Fancy Watches
[a ramble on time]

I've noticed that lately, watches have gotten bigger…more ponderous.

I remember when they were more discreet, elegant in thinness and under- stated in size….

but not these babies.

I'm looking at a few while Diane shops.

I pick one up.

I have no intentions of purchasing it…really…

not just for aesthetic reasons, but at 73 I hardly need one of these behemoths.

But they really do have easy to read numbers…hmm…

But hell, I am already too aware of what yawns before me with every breath and step I take.

Oh wow…this one has a pedometer on it…

And it even tells you how many calories…

but I don't need some kitschy ostentation to remind me that "*tempus fugit*"!

I lift one of them: a huge, heavy silver thing with three separate time dials.

Heh...its 10:30 AM in Paris, 3 PM in Amsterdam and...

But you can program it for just about any city in any time zone.

It tracts the inside temperature, the latitude and longitude of wherever I find myself in one of my many Indiana Jones adventures...and of course the day and month...the current cycles of the moon...

in case I'm of the lupine persuasion...and a lot of other technical numbers and measurements that baffle me.

My lower brain stem, that old reptilian cortex that is attracted by all shiny things, suddenly overwhelms my more evolved neo-cortex...

I want it! I want it!

I'm attracted by a bold, macho one that must come with at least a machete or some instrument of destruction. I imagine the big sweaty, muscle guys that would wear watches like this.

Another one has some exotic, scientific gimmickry that would give a super nerd a super woody.

It has the heft of a concrete brick and exhibits the awkward, self-conscious posturing of an adolescent.

It's trying way too hard.

Desire falters.

I lay it down on the velvet.

Karen, the pleasant young woman in charge of this section, walks over and offers to show me others.

Attempting to exhibit a more technical acumen than my original, reflexive, childish associations, I inquire about its power source.

"Actually it has a very long lasting battery"…she thinks for a moment… *"Sort of like the one I have in my pacemaker."*

She lays one hand unconsciously across her heart.

I snapped back to attention.

I thanked her, and walked away to find a better use for my remaining time.

Small Comforts
[a ramble on aging]

At my age, I'm no longer bothered by the glandular imperatives of youth...read *"Horny"*.

It was fun-while it lasted but now it all seems sort of ridiculous... all that huffing and puffing.

Besides...I always felt-usually afterwards- that there had to be something else, something "more".

But not even this book will get me "more" of what I need...and you know what I'm talking about!

No amount of notoriety will get you "more" of the only commodity that counts.

DaVinci's still dead...

as the tourists from Kansas City crowd around the Mona Lisa.

"Didn't realize it was so...well...so small."

So is *Elvis*...

"And don't forget to stop off at the Graceland gift shop for your memento of the King."

Fame ... the ultimate fraud.

I've managed to ignore all the clichés and clever subterfuges used to mitigate my current slide into old age.

Don't get me wrong; I'm digging my heels in, but like a man on the slippery slide into the alligator pit…the outcome is certain.

Getting old is a bitch…aside from being able to buy cheaper movie tickets.

Now I am finally sitting quietly by this garden.

It took such a long time to get here…

and so much stumbling along the way.

Now I realize that my whole life was an attempt to avoid… getting here.

This is not how I imagined "cool"…

But now I'm an old man, sitting in the midst of these small comforts: twittering birds, ringing chimes, this warm, fickle wind that sets the Tibetan flags in motion… and best of all… you, my love, moving among your flowers and plants, administering to them with those knowing hands.

Waiting for the Storm
[a ramble on "The Big One"]

We are waiting for the winds.

On the radio, the heralds of doom are announcing the apocalypse every few minutes:

This is going to be a big one... and we should brace ourselves:

Remove all the lawn furniture; take down the bird feeders, anything that could become a lethal projectile.

I have a momentary image of being impaled by the large lawn umbrella by the garden.

That comes down first.

There is a sacred place in the center of every fear, an opportunity to come closer to something essential ...

if we have the courage to confront its scary unpredictability.

This existence seldom fits into our comfortable narratives ...

so we are excited and terrified by these impending disturbances in our deadening routines.

The storm will come and pass, leaving and taking what it will...

and we will sink back into a practiced amnesia where we are safe from the chaos of wind and rain...

until the next one...that really could be "The Big One".

"Tomano"

[a rant on "the significance of the trivial"]

You know those red, pulpy slices you get in your salad in most restaurants-even in the height of the summer harvests?

They taste like Cardboard and/ or congealed saw dust…if you're lucky?

Well those are <u>not</u> tomatoes!

They're fakes…imposters… institutional "*tomanos.*"

Yes, I made the word up because I find this common, modern, gustatory perversion really offensive; for me it is symbolic of many things that have gone awry in our culture.

Some of you may be saying: *"Can't he find something more important to write about besides this triviality?"*

But as the old adage states: "the devil's in the details."

I believe our willingness to accept mediocrity is indicative of a dangerous decline in our fundamental tastes and standards.

We have been conditioned to service our desires before anything else.

We can no longer differentiate the relative quality of things.

We no longer seem to be able to discern the "good" from the "bad", and most importantly -discern simple truth from blatant bullshit.

Regard the current political circus.

We do not accept that all things- even a tomato- need to ripen in their own time.

The idea of limitations, of non-availability is unacceptable.

We want it when we want it.

There may be no argument about "taste", but its absence is obvious.

My Mother's Son
[a ramble on vanity]

When Simone, my volatile French mother finally exited this life, it was in her usual dramatic fashion: refusing to accept her less than ambulatory state, she lost her balance and fell, striking her head to begin her departure.

At 90, it had been a long and varied trip from the arrondissements of Paris to the suburbs of Monterey, California.

It was my task – being the only child – to clean and sell her house.

Hercules had nothing on me.

Faced with this daunting task, I began with her capacious bathroom: a wall of mirrors lined with dozens of mysterious, multicolored bottles of unguents and potions she used in her frantic attempts to allay the cruel onslaughts of time.

If you saw her picture when she was a young mademoiselle, you'd understand.

Simone was a "knock-out".

This room was like the secret alcove of a medieval alchemist.

I held each bottle and read the labels that promised mysterious, magic ingrediants that would erase the onslaughts of time.

This triggered one of my reflexive, pretentious, internal monologues on our cultural preoccupations with youth and beauty and our terrors of aging and death.

I congratulated myself that I had – through all the various spiritual disciplines I had practiced -transcended such obsessions and fears.

Then I caught a reflection of my aging countenance in one of her mirrors and reflexively wondered if perhaps there might be some mitigation- among this array of slickly labeled containers-some possible, efficacious tactic to arrest my own disintegration and accelerating revolutions around the dismal drain of time.

I was my mother's son.

Not Buying

[a rant concerning "anthropomorphism"]

anthropomorphism: the attribution of a human form, human characteristics, or human behavior to nonhuman things, e.g. deities in mythology and animals in children's stories like... Zeus, Apollo, Thor, Gumby, Winnie the Pooh, Mickey Mouse ...

A sign outside a local church: *"God knows what you're thinking and doing every moment."*

I've been around long enough to have witnessed many such affirmations of the deity's super hero powers.

It's always struck me as incredibly invasive and presumptuous...

like Super Man checking Lois out with his x-ray vision.

Every murderous thought carried into action by every depraved maniac from Genghis Khan, Jack the Ripper, to your next door neighbor....who everyone thought was such a sweet man...until they found the children's bones buried in his cellar...

and *"HE"* knew all about it?

Every rapist, murderer, torturer, molester who fills the morning news....

all the strident pleas for mercy in the cattle cars on their way to chimneys, all their burnt corpses in the ovens...just flies on the windscreen...the hurricanes and tsunamis that wipe us away by the thousands, plagues, starvation, genetic defects, earth quakes, accidents, AIDS, Hiroshima, a random asteroid...and so on.

And "*HE*" knows… knew…

but "*HE*" did nothing, nada, zilch?

Yeah, yeah, I'm familiar with the legal and philosophical jargon of the apologists.

"*HE*" won't interfere with our so called "*free will*": that vague, over estimated abstraction of faulty, fried wires and sparking circuits…

all this carnage within the context of a brutal, wind-up world that "*HE*" has created.

I'm sorry, but in what way does this slaughterhouse of deranged psychopaths make any "sense" to you?

And in spite of all this brutality and horror, you still hear those who preach about a loving, caring Super Conscious Being, a comforting, loving father figure/favorite uncle who you can talk to, and who <u>really</u>, <u>really</u> loves you… but… who will condemn you to eternal agonies of torment for playing with your "willy".

If "*HE*" is having a good day…

"*HE*" might cure your cancer.

"*HE*" might even fix the game so your team wins.

But if something is cosmologically awry, causing "*HIM*" to deal with a colossal hair across his ethereal posterior…

You're out of luck!

But he is reported to be a bit fickle at times so you never know.

I'm sorry but this is a form of pathological *anthropomorphism*…

a recurrent cartoon we play in our heads...

a mirror in which we only see our needs and fears...

a glitch in the gears...

a pathetic attempt to account for chance and impermanence...

Sorry... but for me the "mysteries" make this life interesting, scary, creative, and a whole bunch of other adjectives I'm not willing to give up for comfort and the illusion of security.

I'm not buying it!

Frenchy

[a ramble on getting a "nickname"]

You cannot give yourself a nick name.

To do so is the height of arrogance and artifice…

and makes you one pretentious asshole.

I received mine in a dormitory room in New Mexico while working at the Albuquerque Indian School.

"Lights out boys"…I announced in my forced, overly authoritative voice.

"Ok Whitey"… was the response from one of the young boys who shared the room with others from the local pueblos that the school serviced.

I deserved it.

I refrained from reacting negatively to my reduction to such a cliché, to such an unimaginative epithet, filled with a whole lot of racist baggage.

To get pissed off would only confirm their initial response to my patronizing tone.

That's what "white people" do when challenged in any way.

But I was hurt!

I felt I wasn't just a "*Whitey*" –or an "*Anglo*", as we were more formally identified in the "genus /specie" nomenclature of "races" in New Mexico.

Thinking back, I realized how typical I had been…

I <u>was</u> "*Whitey*"!

I had made so many arrogant assumptions and mistakes with these kids.

Seven pueblos sent their students here…

and each pueblo had its own culture, rituals, religions…and jokes.

So I responded with *"I'm not white… I'm French!"*

"Ok…Frenchy, Frenchy"… the whole room erupted with shouts and laughter…and it felt right, perfect, as a matter of fact.

Born in Paris France in 1942, my father in the French Republican Guard…murdered by the Gestapo a week after I was born…my mother's name: *Simone*…yes *Simone*…you don't get more French than that.

So "*Frenchy*" it was …and I came in the next day wearing a black beret.

They wore their tribal regalia; I wore mine.

And we got along better than before because we humans can get it right when we understand our own origins and appreciate one another's uniqueness.

I know…I'm preaching…but that was what I learned and I'm telling it.

No…you can't give yourself a nickname…but you might be lucky enough to get one you can live with…one that reminds you of who you really are…

and makes you wonder about what you don't know about others.

That's my story and I'm sticking to it!

"Au revoir."

Hopeless

So finally –I am done with "hope"…and "hope" is done with me.

What a relief to have survived the fickle currents of impulse and desire.

But I admit that I have often wondered if I could have achieved something …well…more?

I'm not talking about having my bust in the Pantheon of Achievements …

or an equestrian statue in the park, a palate for the pigeons… nothing like that.

But I was hoping to have accomplished …well… more. Of what…I'm not sure.

I am jolted back to reality by the passing of some hyper testosterone teenager with his 1000 watt stereo jacked up to a rivet rattling volume.

I am present again.

Today, the garishly colored pinwheels spin wildly on their garden posts. They whir and rattle crazily.

Our tattered, Tibetan flag snaps its rain effaced Sanskrit prayers into the warming, July air.

The wind lifts the undersides of leaves.

They catch the sun, blazing red and silver.

I am stunned.

So much beauty that I missed along the way.

The Gladiolas and garden phlox dance and writhe with each breeze.

The statue of the meditating Buddha I gave you so long ago has dulled from its once ruby luster into an ashen gray. You planted thyme all around it and its tiny, purple blossoms have spread everywhere; it's appropriate on so many levels.

Behind me the traffic hums, the guttural low slung rumble of a passing motorcycle adding its abrasive bass to the higher register of the chimes.

The distant bark of a dog, the growl of a chainsaw, the hum of a lawnmower, steaks on the grill next door, a mélange of smells and sounds...

and I'm in the middle of it all... watching you move about your garden with your customary grace while the tomatoes ripen, the Morning Glories climb, the peppers grow, and the beans keep reaching...

What's to hope for?

"Is Anybody Listening?"
[A ramble on" prayer"]

Again, this was a question written on the board outside a local church. I do get a lot of material this way.

Aside from its arrogance and presumptuous tone, I was impressed with the outrageous nature of the question's intent.

I don't believe the irony was intended since it is the primary inquiry at the heart of atheism: *"Is anybody listening?"*

Of course synchronicity and coincidence can be infinitely interpreted…

so if you choose to knock two coconut shells together to successfully chase away the saber tooth tigers …go to it!

Besides…when you get what you want… *"HE"* really was listening.

When you don't… *"HE"* had other plans

"HE's" "mysterious" you know… so suck it up!

I realize that this attitude is going to set off a firestorm in the ranks of the "true believers" who have honed and polished their certitudes and counter arguments to repel the possibility that no one, no-thing… is "out there"… listening…to us.

I mean all we do down here is pray…and hope – usually "HE"- is listening.

You can believe what you want, but the evidence is monumental for the general deafness, the consistent lack of response to our strident pleas for some recognition from some imagined orchestrator.

I remember reading years ago about the nature of the "bicameral mind"; apparently, there was a time when our hemispheres were not wired too tight and the nascent electrical circuitry between them often manifested as "voices"…heard in our heads…often interpreted as communication with the deity…or deities. We still have people who claim that they hear "*the voice of God*".

They're usually running for office.

Now that most of us no longer hear these "voices"… is there possibly another level of cerebral integration that we need to seriously explore?

As *Jack Gurney [the 14 the Earl of Gurney]* responded to the question of why he had concluded that he was God: *"I find that when I pray- I'm talking to myself." [Peter O'Toole- "The Ruling Class"]*

Is anybody listening?"

Well, that's up to you!

Every day is Yellowstone
[a short ramble on uncertainty]

It's been all over the Internet... or so I've been told. The deer and elk are leaving Yellowstone in herds. There have even been a few low-grade earthquakes, perhaps premonitions of worse to come.

Scientists have been warning of an overdue eruption of a massive caldera in this area... A world killer... If it ever comes to that: our world would be shrouded for decades under a murdering, suffocating ash – and that would be that...at least for a while until another species gave it a go.

But the universe would barely shudder. We would be one more disappearing light in an ocean of black.

When we winked out -at least temporarily for the planet, but permanently for us-would other conscious beings somewhere speculate about us?

Was there intelligent life there?

I've read that over 95% of all life forms that have inhabited this planet eventually became extinct.

But of course that won't happen to us because we are "special".

So many questions... So few absolutes... But one thing is certain:

every day is Yellowstone when you feel the trembling beneath your feet.

And beyond

[a ramble on presumption]

There's a bus that passes by the window where we have breakfast on some early mornings.

The bus has an ad in large, bold letters from a local hospital. It's on both sides and the back:

"From birth to midlife and beyond"

Now both in our 70s, we are entering the suburbs of the "beyond" with greater rapidity than we like.

That's why we take the time to have breakfast together and actually talk to each other… no cell phones

But this distracting ad- almost calling for a sonorous swirl of pipe organ- is obtrusive.

It's irritating.

The bus seems to pass by every 15 min. We must be on its route.

All we want to do is to drink our coffee and talk. We don't need to be distracted by reminders of our incipient departures… and what may… or may not… lie beyond.

Can't we just forget about it for a moment…please… if you don't mind?

Of all the poetic devices- like "departures"- euphemisms are potentially the most troublesome… if not downright devious.

It's the blarney of Wall Street… the cloying cloud of perfume attempting to hide the vile stench of body odor and farts in the court of Louis XIV.

Its purpose is usually to convince you of the romance, the adventure, the awesomeness… of some form of bullshit they want you to buy … or believe.

So this ad is an annoying obfuscation and a pathetic, transparent attempt to smooth over the unknown with a stab of lame, poetic rhetoric.

We know what *"birth"* and *"midlife"* are all about – we've been there – but the *"beyond"* starts trespassing on territory where none in flesh and form have been…yet.

This is the domain of shamans and fakirs. We have plenty of those.

They will promise you anything if you just buy into their cosmology and permutations of *Disneyland*.

This hospital – besides filling out the requisite paper work on our demise-has no business with the *"beyond"*!

So shut the hell up?

"Something After"

We are the haunted specie. I don't believe I'm being overly dramatic to say this.

Well...maybe just a bit, but I do believe that the sense of our mortality underlies just about everything we do and think, either consciously...or not. The "ghost of the end" never leaves us alone for very long, no matter how adept we get at disguising it with some form of camouflage.

Fear is the great compromiser and we are often tempted to grab ferociously at any "*silver ring*" on this wonderful, often ridiculous and terrifying "merry-go-round".

The fear of impermanence, of uncertainty has spawned endless "belief systems" having to do with fanciful forms of continuance and the alleviation of anxiety.

Buddhism attempts to express the simple fact that all composite beings/things tend toward dissolution, whether it's flesh or the very planet we inhabit; there are no exceptions.

Our scientists refer to this as "*entropy.*"

It is cosmic and eternal.

The Buddhists refer to this as "The Dharma"...the way things are...not the way we'd like them to be.

In the spirit of this reality, it has <u>not</u> been my purpose to convince you of anything or to impose my "template" on your experiences.

These were thoughts I had to get out. *[You should try it sometime.]*

I've come to believe that there is little that we truly know.

Besides the fact and experience of impermanence, we have few impeccably certain answers to the ultimate questions of meaning and purpose.

I realize how difficult this "path" is for most people, but- as previously stated- it was not my purpose to proselytize or preach.

It would be the ultimate hypocrisy for me to believe that I have the last, true "*Story on Truth*"…

nor do I see this as some kind of "heroic" posture towards the standardized "belief systems."

But I do admit to reaching out to those who, like me, find those "systems" inadequate and too fraught with contradictions.

I will accept no "system" where there seems to be a requisite necessity for the violation of critical analysis.

I do not believe that there is an impermeable "wall" between "Mystery" and "Reason."

"Reason" explores "Mystery" and just when it seems a "fait accompli" *[I'm French, remember?]*…

it becomes like those Russian Icons that keep revealing yet another one inside…and another one inside of that…and so on.

I think that this is what's really, truly "cool"…the permanence of change…inside impermanence.

Think about it…and come to your own conclusions; you've just read some of mine.

[Thanks...by the way.]

My "salvation" has been through creativity: teaching, writing, singing, composing, and playing my instruments.

To have lived a life of creative activity is enough for me. I'm open to "surprises", but not sufficiently so to confuse imaginings with objective truth.

I wrote the best poetry and songs I could. As of this moment-aside from a few people- I am unknown and I am at peace with this. Fame is the ultimate fraud and too often a misguided attempt to avoid the "shipwreck".

Just as we can never be rich enough...we can never be famous enough.

I believe that there is no one answer to the perpetual conundrum of purpose and meaning; I know...hardly original. But let me add my "footprints" on this well traveled "beach".

I guess what I've been saying is: we are our own hand <u>and</u> clay. I believe that there is nothing outside of ourselves that will automatically give us "the answer".

There are just some "paths" that are more productive to our freedom and joy than others.

This "ship" is going down. There will be no last minute rescue. This flesh <u>is</u> a shipwreck and no amount of frantic bailing will evade that fact.

It would be great if there were "more" than this short span of breathing space...that when we fizzle out, we would find ourselves in rolling fields of ineffable beauty.

To be honest…I'm not totally ruling it out.

But would it be that great to be that same "self"… "you"… forever?

I wish you success in the pursuit of whatever "singing" does it for you.

Song Lyrics

Originally, I was going to include a CD with *"Singing in the Lifeboats"* but that was going to be a bit cumbersome and make the book too expensive; so if any of the included lyrics intrigue you, you can go to:

Jerrylagadec.bandcamp.com

You'll be able to sample the ones you like and download them. Some songs are solo [just me and my guitar and harp]. Some are collaborative efforts with some great musicians.

Before I started writing poetry, rambles and rants…I wrote song lyrics. I spent years refining them. I hope a few catch your interest.

NOTE: If you would like to hear some of the poetry from *Walking with Basho* recited over the musical compositions of Steve Coburn and Frederick Rose, go to: ***glagadec.com***

Also, songs **#2, #5, and #10**, besides being tracks from ***The Ferocity of Time*** CD, are also part of the Musical- ***SHAMAN;*** if this is of interest to you, go to : ***shamanplay.com*** for samples of the libretto and the orchestral arrangements of these pieces and many others.

We are searching for theater groups to use ***SHAMAN;*** the introduction in the libretto section of the web site will explain in greater detail. You can reach me at glagadec@juno.com …or leave a message at any of the other web sites above.

#1: Highway 103 –
from *"Waiting for the Rapture-jerry on guitar and vocals"*

V1: One night- outside of Denver– on Highway- 103.
Stopped –picked up a stranger- who told this tale to me:
About a young, Moroccan man –in Casablanca long- ago
Who played guitar- in a Romani band-and sang so soft and- low…
B1: So mesmerized- she could not help herself…
Looked in his eyes-he took her someplace else.

V2: It might- have been his eyes- his voice- his caress,
His cool hands on her warm thighs- his lips- on her neck.
[But][She woke up- enraptured- entranced by the- moon.
Totally captured -by his haunting, gypsy- tune…
B2: So hypnotized- she could not -helpherself.
Looked in his eyes- he- took her someplace else.

V3: Now- she works the truck stops- on Highway- 103.
They all want -what she's got-but they won't get it for free…
But it's still- so damn- annoying- when there's nothing you can- do!
No use -in ignoring- this need that feeds on- you.
B3: So mesmerized- you just can't help yourself…
Look in her eyes- she'll take you someplace else.

V4: When time means next to- nothing – well nothing- holds a- thrill
[it's] A gnawing kind of hungering-a hole you'll never- fill.
[and] it's not the life she- had in mind- this aversion to the -light
These bullet ridden- high way signs- this insatiable -appetite.
B4: So mesmerized- I could not- help- my-self.
Looked in her eyes- she took me someplace else…

V5: Woke up- feelin' haggered- disoriented- drained.
   She said "I know you're tired-and I'm the one to- blame…
   but I just got too lonely- couldn't take it any-more.
   I really needed – some company… then she vanished out the- door.
   B5: They give her rides—she drops down to her knees
      Then look surprised- when she smiles and shows her teeth…

V6: One more unsolved mystery – on Highway 103
   One more exit to eternity- on Highway 103…
   Cause no one- ever rides for free-on Highway 103…
   And that's where she still waits for me-on highway 103. [repeat- fade]

#2: <u>The Ferocity of Time-</u>

*from "The Ferocity of Time"-Jerry on vocals and guitar; Dana Wilkinson on orchestral arrangements. [from **Shaman**- the musical: shamanplay.com]*

V1: The night is so cold-
　　It's the season.
　　The stars look so old-
　　What's the reason?
　　That I'm walkin' down some street
　　With the echos of my feet.
　　　　B: *It's the velocity of time*
　　　　　　It's the ferocity of time.

V2: I saw his face
　　Through that window.
　　His sad old face
　　On that pillow.
　　Watched the moonlight touch his hair.
　　Smelled the flowers everywhere
　　　　B: *[repeat]*

V3: Don't you think time
　　Is so vicious?
　　I know it must sound
　　Superstitious-
　　That I turn all the clocks to the wall
　　And count the sand as it falls.

B: *It's the ferocity of time- [repeat over and over to fade to...]*
  They say this life's just a shadow-
  Of the real thing yet to come-
  And all our suffering and our sorrow
  Will just vanish and be gone
  From the darkness to a bright light
  When the Endless has begun-
  "Gonna rise up...rise up singin'" [repeat to fade]

#3: Waiting for the Rapture-
from *"Waiting for the Rapture"*-
Jerry on guitar and voice.

V1.[A] Pentecostal church- deep in Georgia woods…
　　Hear the people prayin'- well… they're in a righteous mood…
　　Askin' Lord- please rain down-your fire and your glory…
　　On the heads of sinners- like you do in Good Book stories.

V2: Reverend Jim is Preachin'- got the Holy spirit…
　　Movin' to the music- Now he's really getting' with it…
　　Reachin' up to heaven- white shirt soakin' wet
　　Shouting "Halleluah" – workingup a holy sweat.
　　B: *Hear- the people- prayin' [singin']- [they're] rockin' and swayin',*
　　the walls-are ringin"
　　The Lord has got them -goin'- got them speaking in tongues-
　　without them knowin'
　　Waiting for the Rapture,-gonna float up through the rafters…
　　Waiting for the Rapture- those bright and greener pastures.

V3: Sister in the front row- got those hungry eyes…
　　Jezebel lipstick- and a red dress hitched too high…
　　Smirkin' and smilin'-squirmin' in her seat
　　Jim is really tryin'- but he can't escape the heat…

V4: The Sheriff found their bodies- in that cheap motel
　　Together now for ever- in the deepest part of hell.
　　A wedding band lay shinin'- in a pool of blood
　　Another man lay dyin'- said he did it all for love.

#4: The Great Escape-
[from *"Waiting for the Rapture"-Jerry* *– vocal and guitar*]

V.1: She wanders- doesn't know where she's going- the sky's grey- soon it's going to start snowing...-calling his name-in every shadow- searching for him- in every window.

The years passed- all their hopes crushed by heart break- her mind's blank, nothing left but a dull ache. They were so young- life was a promise- then things went wrong- a total, complete mess.

B1

V2: A blind man's-shining shoes on the corner- his hands move- with a rhythm and wild blur. -He's far away- miles from the city- hearing the waves- in sunny Tahiti.

The wind blows- all the old news around him-and he knows- that tomorrow is Sunday.

He'll go to the Bronx to visit his mother- she'll fix him some lunch- then weep for his father.

B1 and B2

B1: *And they dream of the great escape- tigers burning for a William Blake*

Natives on hot tropic sands- striking poses for a Paul Gaugain.

B2: Of Lotto numbers in the night-that will lift them up into the light...

of parting thighs- and waiting lips-of roulette wheels and exotic trips...

in limousines- on sailing ships.....that take them away.

V3.Her name tag- says to call her Patricia- she works for- her older brother and sister.

-In an old diner car- pouring strong coffee- next to a bar- full of hookers and junkies.

She dreams that- soon a man will come save her-they'll drive off- in a Cadillac chauffeured by a driver in black- with a French accent- They'll never look back-disappear in the traffic.

V4: He goes down-to the park, feeds the pigeons-then stops off-to his church for religion.

He kneels in the back-mumbling his rosary-he wants to believe-but it just isn't easy.

His wife's gone- the cancer just took her-his heart' stone- no one's got any answers.

Then he goes home-for a micro-wave dinner-he eats all alone-like some kind of prisoner.

B:[repeat] *And they dream...*

#5: Road Kill-

*from "The Ferocity of Time" -Jerry-
vocal and guitar; George Johnson–Bass;
Phil Oliver-drums- Paul Curran- Sax]
also from **SHAMAN** –shamanplay.com*

V1: Faces in a window- cigarette in a hand
   Neon, blood, and sirens-Silhouette of a man.
   Jazz floating down from somewhere- It sounds like "The Train"
   Heavy with some sorrow- marinated in pain.
   B: One more stain of road kill in the street.
   This time no one's landing on their feet

V2: She said she got religion- but it don't mean a thing.
   It's only superstition- and you know what that brings…
   You lose your soul to passion. You're mind is not straight.
   No thought before the action- you're a victim of fate.
   B: [repeat]

V3: Chalk lines on the sidewalk- a crowd gathers round.
   Flashbulbs in a dead eye-a pantomime clown.
   Just another pusher-who crossed someone's line.
   Just another hooker- layin' there dyin'.
   B: [repeat]

#6: Natasha-
from"Waiting for the Rapture"-
Jerry- vocals and baritone guitar]

V1: When they came for you- you just turned 22- you said- good-bye to your friends.

You were so naïve- they led you to believe- this was – a start- and not an end.

B1: Just like a fly- caught on their dark web.
You wanna die- but you're already dead.

V2: Movie magazines- with their exotic scenes- really- played hell with your head.

Then their dreams turned stale- their lights began to fail- [now] you're flat- on your back in bed.

B1: [repeat]
Chorus: Natasha- what will you do?
Natasha- they're killing you.

V3. Well they kept you high- sold you to any guy- you're gone and nowhere to be found.

And you pray each day- you could just get away- you scream- but you don't make a sound.

B1: [repeat
Chorus:[repeat]

V4. When they used you up- you finally had enough–the time for payback's finally come!

What a big surprise- the panic filled their eyes- where- did she get that gun?

B: Now- you are stumblin'-out into the light.
Can't keep from smilin'-no more spider bites.
Chorus: Natasha- you finally won- Natasha- you got a gun [repeat]

#7: 47 Days-
from "Waiting for the Rapture" - Jerry-vocals and harp]

V1: Call me Ishmael – I went off to sea.
   An abalone shell – ....whispered out to me...
   "Set your sails my son – catch a vagrant wind
   You could be the one –.... to spot that devil's fin.

B: *He mesmerized us- crawled up in our brains*
   He hypnotized us –drove us all insane.

V2: 47 days – since I saw the coast
   47 days –.... driftin' in this boat.
   47 days – this could be the last.
   47 days – ....I scratch'em on the mast.

B2: *The Devil rides a pure white whale*
   with crushing teeth- and a forked tail.
   He swallows up –drowned sailor's souls
   And drags them down.... to the deep, dark cold.

V3: A tortured, crippled man – a mangled misery
   [with]his harpoon in his hand –he cursed his history:
   The rending of his flesh – that left him for a wreck.
   Beating on his chest –he limped across the deck.

B: *His eyes burned hotter- than two blazing suns*
   He passed a bottle –.... of strong Jamaican rum.

V4: He hammered on the mast- nailed his gold doubloon...
   Winds blew wild and fast....- as he waved his black harpoon.
   Burning with desire-compelled by mindless rage...
   We caught his hate and fire-....just players on his stage.

B2: The timbers screamed- saw the jaws of hell...
Got thrown overboard-as the rigging fell
Watched him climb- the whale's broad back...
With a stab of steel —he turned the waters black.

V5: 47 days – totally alone
47 days- reduced to skin and bone.
47 days – can't escape his curse
47 days –haunted by his words.

B: I'm barely breathin'- is that a sail ahead?
Am I hallucinatin'- and almost dead.
This boat's a coffin-it was my friend's.
I think it's leakin'-.... this could be the end...[repeat]

#8- Hotel Dolorosa –
from "*Waiting for the Rapture*"-jerry- guitar and vocal

V1: Dirty, drafty, dim-lit halls
Nasty, stale, burnt hot-plate
smells
Dingy, stained graffiti walls
In this border town hotel.

V2: I got a dizzy, bird's eye view
Of a neon sign below.
Flashing yellow, green and blue
As the gringos come and go…

V3: Fallen down on hard luck
times-
Strung-out on the wheel of
pain
Wasted, burnt-out, broken
minds.
Weeping, wailing and
insane

V4: Spirits haunt the thread-
bare floors.
Begging for some quick
relief.
Scratching on the chain
locked doors
Of liars, lovers, fools, and
thieves.

*The Hotel Dolorosa
Is where I live now.
The Hotel Dolorosa-
In this Mexican town
The Hotel Dolorosa…
You can use any name…*

B1:*[when] You're tortured by*
   yearning
   For someone not there
   Bare light bulbs burning
   In the hot sticky air.
   Angry flies buzzing
   On strips everywhere
   Worn out whores working
   All the alleys and stairs

B 2: *[when] You're tortured by*
   longing
   For what's in the past
   Wasting time wanting
   hat'cha never can have.
   Sad guitar crying
   In some room below
   Drunken voice prayin'
   Lord, please save my soul

#9- Three Lovers –
from *"Waiting for the Rapture"*-Jerry- guitar and vocals

V1: Two cigarettes- burning holes in the night.
    68 Corvette- disappearing from sight.
    Late rendezvous- at the Star-Lite Motel.
    Me, him and you- at the Star-Lite Motel.

V2: So close behind- smell your strong, cheap perfume.
    You drop the blinds- on that crumby back room.
    Late rendezvous- at the Star-Lite motel.
    Me, him and you- at the Star- Lite motel.

B1: *And in your quick surrender- I know you don't remember—[but]*
    that this is where we met!
    Smoky eyed and schemin'—a busy spider weavin'- but you ain't
    seen nothin' yet!

V3: This trigger's ice-like your heart- it's jet black.
    I pull it twice –now there's no turnin' back.
    Last rendezvous- at the Star-Lite Motel.
    Me, him and you- at the Star-Lite motel.

V4: The barrel's hot – the blood's soakin' the sheets.
    With one more shot -this melo-drama's complete.
    The sirens scream- to the Star-Lite motel.
    A tabloid scene- at the Star-Lite motel.

B2: *They'll read about it in the paper- forget about it later- when*
    there's something new to tell.
    I know the cops are comin'- I hear their muffled runnin'-on my
    way to hell.

#10- The Swimmers –

from *"The Ferocity of Time"- jerry on vocals and, guitar- also from* **SHAMAN**- *shamanplay.com*

V1: This ocean seems much larger
    And deeper than before...
    And my arms are getting tired...
    I cannot see the shore

B: *So many islands- we've caught our breath upon...*
   So many miles- through storms and winds and sun...
   But I will swim with you...I will dive with you until we drown.

V2: These waves seem so much higher...
    Or is it just the light...
    Salvation seems much farther
    And we're swimming into night...

B: *[repeat]*

V3: Down on the bottom...
    It all turns back to pearl...
    No more the sound of...
    The anger of this world...

B:*[repeat]*

V4: Out of this harbor where no one ever stays
    The waves from that far shore will carry us away
    But I will swim with you- I will dive with you-until we drown.

Printed in the United States
By Bookmasters